Straight
from the
Heart
for DAD

Straight From the Heart for Dad

by
Richard Exley

Tulsa, Oklahoma

Straight From the Heart for Dad
ISBN 1-56292-093-6
Copyright © 1995 by Richard Exley
P.O. Box 54744
Tulsa, Oklahoma 74155

Published by Honor Books
P.O. Box 55388
Tulsa, Oklahoma 74155

Presented to:

Dad Bikker

On the Occasion of:

Christmas

Presented by:

Jeremy, Jacqueline, Steven

Date:

December 23, ~~99~~ 2000

DEDICATION

*To Dick Exley and
Ben Roy Wallace*

Contents

An Awesome Responsibility

"*Today you became a father.... and you find yourself reflecting, for the first time, on what an awesome responsibility it is to parent a child.*"

Chapter 1

∽

An Awesome Responsibility

*T*oday you became a father. After nine months of waiting, it finally happened: your wife presented you with an eight-pound, seven-ounce baby boy.

Now you are home, alone in the house, and it is late, but you are too excited to sleep. Slowly the weariness sets in, and you find yourself reflecting, for the first time, on what an awesome responsibility it is to parent a child. Suddenly, you are filled with an overwhelming appreciation for your parents, especially your dad.

Thinking about him now, you realize that he wasn't a man much given to words. Not once did he sit down with you and impart some moral principle or life lesson. Yet, you realize, almost everything you know about life and godliness you learned from him. Not so much from the things he said, but from the way he lived.

You remember how resourceful he was, how he always serviced his own cars, repaired your mom's old Maytag rather than call a service man and remodeled your childhood home when he finally had the money to do it. In addition, he was a willing helper to your mother, who had her hands more than full with four rowdy kids. From him you learned to be a servant-leader years before that phrase was coined.

As a nurturing father, he was second to none. In the evenings, after supper, he hit you flies and played catch with you for hours. When you finally became involved in organized sports, he never missed a game, although you were only a mediocre athlete and seldom saw any action. He took you fishing each summer and taught you to hunt and enjoy the great outdoors. In short, he was never too busy to spend time with you.

Most of all, you remember how much he loved God and the way he cared about people. Never was he too busy to lend a helping hand.

When you were maybe five or six years old, a close friend of the family died suddenly of a brain tumor, leaving his wife and two small children nearly destitute. Shortly after the funeral they were forced to relocate to more affordable housing. Unfortunately, the only thing they could find was a small house in desperate need of repair.

When your dad learned of their predicament, he offered his handyman skills. Sometimes you and your mother accompanied him, but mostly he worked alone, night after night. He replaced the faulty wiring, repaired the leaky plumbing and built new cupboards for the kitchen.

When he had finally finished, that young widow and her two children had a small but comfortable place to call home. More important, they knew that they were not alone, that God had not abandoned them.

Then there's the time he invited a homeless family to spend the night. Without giving them a chance to refuse, he insisted that they follow him home. Your mother made supper for them, although it was long past supper time, and as she put together a simple meal of homemade bread, fried potatoes and ham, the kitchen filled with friendly smells.

You remember following your dad down into the half-finished basement where you collected two quarts of home-canned peaches for dessert. As you ascended the stairs, you distinctly remember hearing the sound of ham sizzling in the skillet. It was a good sound, friendly and comforting. Since that night it has always sounded like love to you.

When the church took pledges for a building program, you recall how your dad found a way to give, even though there wasn't an extra cent in the family budget. Night after night he donned his coveralls and made his way to a collection of discarded machinery rusting behind your uncle's shop.

Often he allowed you to accompany him, and you watched in wonder as the acetylene hissed to life and the blowtorch stabbed the darkness with a bright blue flame. Adjusting his goggles, he bent to the task, and a shower of sparks danced in the darkness like a stampede of fireflies. Beneath his torch the discarded machinery slowly became scrap metal, which could be sold and the money used to help remodel the church building.

Yes, you conclude, your dad was a resourceful man, and a wonderful role model.

You can never remember hearing him curse, and you seldom heard him complain, but you do remember hearing him pray.

Many a morning you awakened in the predawn darkness to the sound of his voice raised in prayer. Throwing back the covers, you tiptoed barefoot down the hall to stand beside the door leading into the living room. As he prayed, you experienced a sense of God's nearness. Never have you felt more loved, more secure, than when he called your name to the Father in prayer.

Whenever you shared some adolescent difficulty, he inevitably said, "Call your mother and let's pray." The three of you would kneel on the bare hardwood floors in front of the frayed couch in the small living room. Together you would lift your voices in prayer. Often the circumstances remained unchanged, but you never failed to feel better by the time you had finished praying.

You have been gone from your father's house several years now, but the values he imparted to you live on. And when you remember the sounds of your childhood, you remember lots of love and laughter, but most of all you remember the sound of your father's voice calling your name in prayer.

Bowing your head, you pray, "Father, may I be to my son all that my father has been to me. And may I impart to him the rich spiritual heritage that my father imparted to me."

CHAPTER

2

Thanks, Dad, for the Memories

"As you lie in bed waiting for sleep to overcome you, your mind drifts back to your own childhood. The thing you remember most is the time your father spent with you."

Chapter 2

∞

Thanks, Dad, for the Memories

*I*t is nearly midnight, and you are exhausted. It has been a long day, and you are not sure an altogether profitable one.

First, there was the picnic in the park, then the trip to the zoo and finally the fireworks at River Park. They were spectacular, but afterwards the traffic was horrendous, and by that time the children were tired and cranky.

Setting the radio alarm, you decide that six o'clock will come far too soon, and then it will be back to the old grind. Perhaps, you think, you should have spent the day relaxing.

As you lie in bed waiting for sleep to overcome you, your mind drifts back to your own childhood. The thing you remember most is the time your father spent with you. Thinking about it now, several memories come to mind — the time he helped you build a clubhouse when you were maybe ten or eleven years old, the first time he took you deer hunting and all the times he played catch with you in the back yard after supper.

Still, no memory is more special than a Fourth of July picnic in Lewis Canyons with a host of relatives.

It was barely noon when you arrived, but already it was uncomfortably hot. Quickly, the men set up folding tables in the scanty shade of an ancient cottonwood, while you helped your cousins place several dark green watermelons in the cold water of a stock tank fed by an underground spring. Later, when you devoured them, their sweet red meat was so cold that the first juicy bites made your teeth ache. Still, for a sunburned boy of eleven, it seemed a small price for such booty.

While the men laid out a place to pitch horseshoes, the ladies covered the tables with red-and-white-checked tablecloths and spread a picnic feast. There were mounds of fried chicken, huge bowls of potato salad, plates of sliced tomatoes and home-canned pickles, baskets of hot rolls and several three-layer chocolate cakes covered with thick frosting.

Once the meal was eaten, the ladies retired to blankets in the shade, while the men pitched horseshoes. You spent the long afternoon exploring the canyons and playing hide-and-seek with your cousins. When hunger and exhaustion finally brought you back, the setting sun was laying long shadows across the canyon floor.

The clear clang of a well-pitched horseshoe drew you like a magnet, and, after gorging yourself on cold chicken and chocolate cake, you turned your attention to the game in progress. Your dad and Uncle Denny were pitching against the preachers — Uncle Ernie and Brother Call, your pastor.

You don't remember who won. You guess it doesn't really matter. What you do remember is fireworks after dark, sparklers and Roman candles, and the long ride home.

Fourth of July celebrations aren't like that anymore. Lewis Canyons are unbearably hot, and the underground spring is brackish and not nearly as cold as you remember. The canyon floor is uneven — not a fit place for a decent horseshoe pit. Maybe it was never any different, except when seen through the eyes of an eleven-year-old boy. For that one day, though, the Fourth of July was all you ever dreamed it would be.

Maybe it will be like that for your children too. Maybe they won't remember being sunburned and tired, or fighting in the car on the way home. Maybe all they will remember is a Fourth of July picnic, a trip to the zoo and a spectacular display of fireworks.

Belatedly, you decide that if twenty years from now they remember today as you remember the Fourth you spent in Lewis Canyons, it will be a day well spent.

Rolling over, you whisper into the darkness, "Thanks, Dad, for the memories."

" ...'A mistake is not all bad if you can learn from it.'"

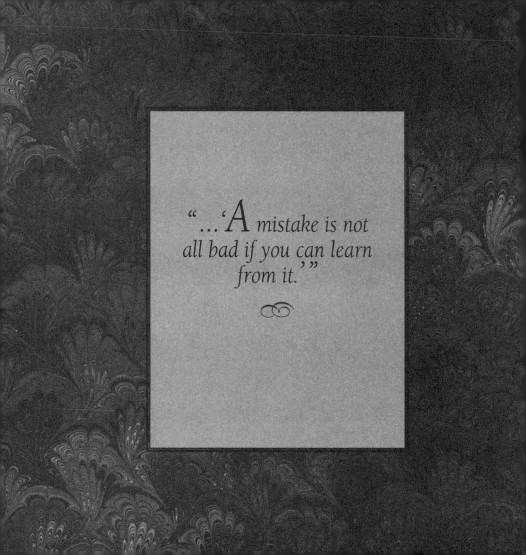

Chapter 3

◌

Next Time

You stand at the window and watch the winter rain beat against the pane. Normally you would feel exhilarated, creative, but not today. This morning you did a shameful thing, and now your regret has turned to self-loathing. You can only conclude that you must be the world's worst father.

You look up as your wife enters the room bearing a cup of steaming coffee. Handing it to you, she joins you at the window. After a minute she asks softly, "Would you like to talk about it?"

Before answering, you replay the scene in your mind. You were teaching a Sunday school class on, of all things, parenting, when you were informed that your six-year-old daughter had walked home, after refusing to go to her class. Excusing yourself, you rushed home, trying to decide how best to handle the situation.

She was sitting on the porch when you arrived, and before you could speak, she said, "I'm not going back to my class, not ever! My teacher's mean."

Without attempting to discover why she was so adamant, you belligerently ordered her to return to Sunday school. She refused, and you spanked her. She still refused, so you spanked her again.

By that time she was crying, and you were exasperated. It had become a battle of wills, and you were determined to win at any cost. Again and again you spanked her, three times, four times, five times. By then you were convinced that the only way you were going to get her in that class was to carry her back, kicking and screaming.

In the end you sent her to her room and returned to the church in time to finish teaching your class. Never have you felt more like a hypocrite.

Taking a sip of your coffee, you say, "As a boy growing up, I had a hot temper, a smart mouth and a soft heart. If you challenged me, I would fight you to the death, but if you appealed to my heart, I was an easy touch. Somehow Dad understood this and refused to become involved in a battle of wills with me. He held his tongue even when it meant losing face in front of others.

"One incident stands out in particular. I was grousing about something, and Dad told me that was enough. My temper flashed, and I told him to shut up or I was going to hit him. Instantly I was ashamed, but youthful pride would not allow me to back down.

"Instead of challenging me then and there, Dad said nothing. Later, when I had cooled down, he had a long talk with me. As he explained how hurt he was, I thought my heart would break. With tears running down my cheeks, I asked him to forgive me. Of course he did, and that incident was never mentioned again.

"Dad had his faults, and he could be almost childish at times, especially about insignificant things. Still, when the chips were down, he had amazing patience and real wisdom."

The room grows quiet, and you notice that your coffee is now cold. Never mind. You aren't in the mood for coffee anyway. You have failed miserably as a parent, and you want to suffer, you want to punish yourself.

After a while your wife speaks: "You probably could have handled things better, but what's done is done. There's nothing to be gained by berating yourself. As you've often told me, 'A mistake is not all bad if you can learn from it.' So let me ask you a question: If that kind of thing should happen again, how will you handle it differently?"

"Next time I'll try to be more in touch with my own feelings. As I think about this morning, I realize that I wasn't really concerned about getting Whitney back in class. I was more concerned about my image, my reputation. I was angry because she was making me look like a poor parent.

"Next time I'll be more aware of Whitney's feelings. I'll give her some time to cool off before I deal with her."

Smiling ruefully, you add, "And most important of all, next time I'll spank her teacher."

You both laugh and then grow quiet as Whitney walks into the living room, rubbing sleep from her eyes. Your heart swells with love for her, and you stretch your arms toward her. Without a moment's hesitation she crawls into your lap, and you hug her tight. She's still Daddy's little girl, and now all is right with the world once more.

CHAPTER

4

The Gift of Yourself

" ... 'the most important thing you can give your children is the gift of yourself. Long after they have forgotten the gifts you bought them, they will remember and cherish the time you spent with them.'"

Chapter 4

❦

The Gift of Yourself

The table is littered with maps, brochures, colored markers, a note pad and a calculator. Frustration has given you a painful headache, and you massage the back of your neck while trying to make the numbers come out right.

No matter how you figure it, you simply cannot afford the family vacation you have been planning for months. The kids will be disappointed. For weeks all they have talked about is going to Disney World in Orlando.

Your wife joins you at the table bearing two mugs of decaf, a recent concession to your growing intolerance for caffeine, especially at night. Perusing your figures, she glances up and says, "That's quite a bit more than we budgeted."

Disgruntled, you nod before adding, "I had no idea it would cost so much to take a family vacation."

"Maybe," she suggests, "if we start putting money into a vacation fund right now, we can go next year."

"My thinking exactly," you reply, "but I sure hate to disappoint the kids. They've really been counting on this."

"Why don't we take them camping somewhere close to home?"

"Are you serious?" you ask in surprise. "I thought you hated camping."

"It's not my favorite thing," she admits, "but the kids will love it."

A slow smile spreads across her face as she entertains a childhood memory. "I was probably nine years old," she reflects wistfully, "the summer my daddy took us camping on the Guadelupe River near New Braunfels, Texas.

"We set up camp on a small bluff overlooking the river, and the next two weeks were as happy as any in my whole life. One sunlit, water-splashed day merged with the next as we swam and played from daylight to dusk. Soon I was as dark as any Indian. To this day, that's the only tan I've ever had."

Sensing her excitement, you encourage her to tell you more. She is only too happy to oblige, and soon she is engrossed in a detailed narrative of life on the Guadelupe. As she talks, something of the child she must have been creeps back into her voice.

"We slept in a tent. Not one of the new nylon kind, but an old-fashioned canvas one. As it heated up during the day, it filled with the pungent odor characteristic of canvas. To me it was an intoxicating smell, one filled with adventure and intimacy. And to this day, the smell of sun-warmed canvas has the power to carry me back to the carefree days of my childhood."

Remembering her almost obsessive concern about dead-bolts and door locks you ask, "Weren't you afraid?"

"Not at all," she answers. "Daddy slept just inside the tent door with a machete at hand. In my eyes he was the bravest man in all the world."

You laugh, and she continues: "We lived in our swimsuits — that is, my sister and I did — taking them off only to sleep. As soon as we got up in the morning, we pulled them on and headed for the river.

"The water was crystal clear and not cold at all. We each had an air mattress, and after carrying them far upstream we would float back down. The river was filled with small rapids which seemed huge to us. As we approached them, we grew sick with dread and anticipation. Inexorably, the current grew stronger, and then it plunged us into the rapids, and we screamed with fearful excitement. Thunder River, or whatever they call the water ride at Disney World, can't compare with that."

"Okay, you've convinced me," you say with a grin. "We'll take the kids camping."

"There were a lot of other families camping too," she rushes on, ignoring your growing impatience, "so we had lots of kids to play with.

Unfortunately, their parents didn't seem to pay much attention to them; consequently, they gravitated toward Dad. He was always thinking up games for all of us to play. One time he showed us how to join hands and cross the river by walking on the rocks. Another day he made a rope swing and showed us how to swing far over the river before letting go and plunging into the water below. All the kids loved him, and he never seemed to tire of playing with us."

She grows quiet, and you begin to clear the table, putting the sundry things away in their proper places. You wash the coffee cups and place them in the drainer to dry. When you are finished, you take her hand and say, "Let's call it a night. It's late."

Though she seems lost in thought, she follows you upstairs and prepares for bed. Once you are in bed together, she says, "Darling, the most important thing you can give your children is the gift of yourself. Long after they have forgotten the gifts you bought them, they will remember and cherish the time you spent with them. I know, because what I remember is not the toys or the dresses my daddy bought me, or even the places we went on vacation, but the things we did together, the time he spent with me."

Giving her a good-night kiss, you promise to spend more time with the children. It won't be easy, but if it is half as important as she thinks it is, then it will worth it.

As you drift toward sleep, you imagine your own children screaming with fearful delight as they shoot the rapids on a bright yellow air mattress.

CHAPTER

5

Father's Day

"*F*atherhood, you conclude, is something of a mixed bag. There are moments of intense joy, and times when you are ready to pull your hair out. Sometimes you laugh, and sometimes you cry."

Chapter 5

∽

Father's Day

Another Father's Day is slowly drawing to a close, and you find yourself reminiscing, reflecting on your own experiences as a father.

Fatherhood, you conclude, is something of a mixed bag. There are moments of intense joy, and times when you are ready to pull your hair out. Sometimes you laugh, and sometimes you cry.

Well did one father put it, "Insanity is hereditary. You get it from your kids."

You are not sentimental by nature, but your oldest daughter is. She will be leaving for college in a couple of months, and sensing that an era in her life is coming to an end, she made a personalized Father's Day card for you. It's a small scrapbook really, containing a photographic history of her eighteen years. Leafing through it now, you allow the pictures to carry you back to an earlier age, to a less hectic time when life was simpler.

There's a picture of your daughter (age five months) on her first Halloween. She's dressed up like a little hobo with freckles painted on her chubby cheeks. How precious she looks sitting in a pile of brightly colored autumn leaves next to a plump, orange pumpkin.

Then there's a picture of her (age eleven months) bundled up like an eskimo, sitting on a picnic table at Twin Lakes. Behind her a snow-capped peak glows orange-red in the late afternoon sun.

In stark contrast the next picture shows her (age thirteen months) in a soft tangerine-colored swimsuit with one shoulder strap falling down. She's sitting in the sand, next to a lake, playing with a large teflon spoon.

Can it be possible that this tiny child is now a young lady of eighteen? It seems that only yesterday you were watching her totter through the house wearing pajama tops and knee socks, nothing else. Now she's elegant in her designer dresses and high heels. Too soon, you realize, you will be walking her down the aisle to present her to the man whose name will replace yours.

Among the photos you discover that she has included a copy of a letter you wrote to her when she was seventeen:

Dear Hailey:

I am 35,000 feet in the air somewhere between Seattle and Anchorage. There are no phones to answer, no deadlines to meet, and no one waiting to see me. Now that I have some time to myself, I find that I am growing nostalgic. Not being one to waste such feelings, I decided to put them in a letter and send it to you.

My memories are like slides which I flash on the screen of my mind. When I do, it all comes back, and it's as real as it was then, maybe more so, because you have to be older to fully appreciate most things.

I remember the day you were born as though it was yesterday. I was only twenty-three and so dumb, at least about things like labor and giving birth. When your mother told me that she was having pains I decided to take care of some business before driving her to the hospital. Without a second thought, I left her alone and drove twenty-eight miles to Lamar to get a license for the car.

They say that God looks after fools and children, and in my case He did. When I finally got back home, almost three hours later, your mother's labor pains were only minutes apart.

Without further delay, I helped her into the car, and away we went. On the way to the hospital I told her that I knew you were going to be a boy. Guaranteed it, in fact!

Well, so much for guarantees...no one would ever mistake you for a boy!

I'm glad I was wrong, for no father ever had a finer daughter, and no mother and daughter were ever closer, were ever better friends, than your mother and you.

The past seventeen years have come and gone more quickly than I could ever have thought possible. One moment you were a babe in arms, then a fresh-faced first-grader, then you were starting junior high. Before we knew it, you were a young lady. Barbie dolls and bicycles gave way to mascara and fashion magazines. Then you got interested in boys, and our house was like Grand Central Station.

In a few weeks you will be starting your senior year, then you will graduate, and be off to college. I'm sorry our time together is almost over, but I wouldn't hold you back for anything. You are such a special person, with so much to give, that I feel a certain responsibility to share you with the world.

Regrets? A few. I wish I had gotten mad less and laughed more. I wish I had had the patience to teach you to ride your bike instead of delegating that responsibility to your mother. And I wish you had learned to drive with a standard transmission rather than an automatic.

Victories? A few. You inherited my love for books. You know how to dream great dreams, and how to work to make those dreams reality. You are resilient, irrepressible, you refuse to stay down. Most of all, you are your own person.

Any last thoughts? A few. When you are grown and have gone out into the world in search of your destiny, I hope you remember how crazy funny I could be when it was just the two of us and I was letting my hair down. I hope you remember how much I loved your mother, and how special I thought she was. I hope you remember how much I loved God, how conscientious I was, and how deeply I cared for people.

Most of all, I want you to remember how special you are to me, and how much I love you. There is nothing you can do, no success or achievement, that will ever make me love you more. I love you, not because of what you do, but just because you are who you are.

Love,

Dad

Your wife comes in as you finish the letter and watches in silence as you swallow past the fist-sized lump in your throat. When you have regained your composure, you ask, "Have you seen this?" When she nods in the affirmative, you say, "She's quite a gal, isn't she?"

Putting her arms around your neck, she kisses you and says, "You're quite a father too, you know."

CHAPTER

6

Real Men, Real Fathers

" '*A* real man... is not embarrassed by his feelings, nor is he afraid to show his emotions.' "

Chapter 6

∽

Real Men, Real Fathers

Lee, a new co-worker and fishing enthusiast, watches as you drop to one knee and place your work-hardened hands on your son's narrow shoulders. Looking him in the eye, you tell him how special he is, and how much you love him. His face glows with pleasure, and he throws himself against your chest. Giving him a parting hug, you say, "Be a big boy now, and take care of Mom while I'm gone."

Picking up a thermos of coffee, you follow Lee toward the pickup which is loaded with camping gear. Once you are on the road, he tentatively asks, "Don't you think your son is getting a little too big for that kind of thing?"

Feigning puzzlement, you ask, "What kind of thing is that?"

"You know what I mean," he stammers uncomfortably, "all that touchy-feelie stuff."

Once more you realize how blessed you are. Although your father was all man, he had no trouble expressing his feelings; consequently, neither do you. According to his way of thinking, emotions were not the private domain of women, but the birthright of all human beings created in the image of God. Many a time he told you, "The ability to express your deepest feelings is not a sign of weakness, but of maturity."

"A real man," he said, "is not embarrassed by his feelings, nor is he afraid to show his emotions."

Your continued silence makes Lee uncomfortable, and he blurts out, "Well, maybe all that affection is all right when a boy is six or seven years old, but when he gets older, things change. My boy stands one inch over six feet tall, he weighs a hundred and seventy-five pounds and he's the star athlete on his high school team. If I gave him a big hug and told him I love him, it would embarrass him to death."

"You might be surprised."

"What do you mean?" he asks.

"It's been my experience," you say, "that inside every hulking young athlete there resides a little boy who hungers for his father's love and approval. No matter how tough he acts, he still longs to hear his daddy praise him."

Lee drives in thoughtful silence for several miles, and you think about your dad. You remember his wisdom and his love. It seemed that he always knew just what to do.

Like the time you missed an important free throw in the final seconds of the district championship game and moped around the house for days. Finally, he said, "Son there is more to life than throwing a round ball through a metal hoop." That's all he said, nothing more. He wasn't making light of your disappointment, just putting it into perspective.

A day or two later he put his arm around your shoulders and told you what a fine young man you were, and how proud he was that you were his son. His faith in you, even in defeat, made all the difference in the world. It was the stuff out of which you built your self-image.

Finally, Lee breaks the silence. "I suppose you're right," he says, "but I wouldn't know how to go about it."

"You can express your love in any number of ways," you explain, "but none is more effective than touching and telling. An arm around the shoulders, a pat on the back, a word of praise from you, will mean more to your son than you will ever know."

"Do you really think so?" he asks.

"Absolutely. The truth is, if your son does not receive your love and approval as he is growing up, he will never become the man he is meant to be. Maybe once in a hundred years a child is ruined by excessive praise, but surely once every minute one dies inside for lack of it."

Lee has heard enough, and he now launches into an animated description of trout fishing in Wyoming. You listen, but on another level you replay your father's praise. Once more you realize how much he contributed to your self-confidence and to your understanding of what it means to be a man and a father.

You are indeed a blessed man.

C H A P T E R

7

*Reflections
at Mid-Life*

"*Thanks, Dad, for believing in me even when I made a mess out of things.*"

Chapter 7

∽◯◯∽

Reflections at Mid-Life

You watch while your eighteen-year-old son stuffs one last arm load of paraphernalia into his compact car as he prepares to leave for Northeastern State University, three hundred miles away.

Already the tiny auto is overflowing with a wide assortment of prized personal possessions. In addition to his clothes and bedding, he has managed to load into it a portable TV, a VCR and a CD player. Of course, he has packed his PC, his guitar, his tennis racket and his basketball.

In truth, his overloaded vehicle resembles nothing quite so much as a low-rider. You are tempted to press your offer to haul some of the stuff up in your car, but you don't. He has made it perfectly clear that he wants to do this himself.

After giving his mother a quick hug, he shakes your hand and drives off without a backward glance. Unfamiliar tears blur your vision as you watch until his car disappears from sight.

Returning to the house, you are assailed with a painfully vivid memory of your own. You haven't thought about it in more than twenty-five years, but now it returns with incriminating clarity.

Like your son, you were only eighteen and fiercely independent when you left for college. Unlike him, you did not have a car of your own, so you had to rely on your parents to transport you.

As soon as you were registered and had your dorm room assigned, you unloaded your things at the curb and bid your folks good-bye. They offered to help you carry your things into the dorm and get your room set up, but you refused. Now you know how they must have felt, and you can't believe you could have been so insensitive.

On an impulse, you decide to write your father. Not to apologize for your insensitivity, there's no need for that, but just to let him know how special he is to you. It would be easier to call, but you have never been very good at expressing your feelings, and you are afraid that you might not be able to say everything that is on your heart.

Putting a pen to paper you write:

Dear Dad:
Today Jeffery left for college. We wanted to drive up with him and help him get settled, but he wouldn't hear of it. Does he remind

you of anyone you know? As they say, "What goes around comes around."

I should have written this letter when I left home and started college, or at least when I graduated, but the truth is, I hadn't lived enough to fully appreciate all you did for me.

I've always loved you and been grateful for all you did for us kids, but I don't think I fully comprehended it until today. Maybe you have to see your kids grow up and leave home before you can fully appreciate all your parents did for you. Anyway, let me share some of the things that stand out in my mind.

Do you remember the Sunday afternoon I rolled the family car? Thankfully, no one was hurt, but the car was pretty banged up, and we had to get a tow truck to pull it out of the ditch. What stands out in my mind is not the accident itself, but the fact that you offered to let me use the car again that evening. Tossing me the keys, you said, "Try not to roll it this time."

By that one act of trust, you taught me not to be afraid to make a mistake. Subconsciously, it has given me the courage to pursue opportunities and to take risks I might otherwise have never dared take.

Thanks, Dad, for believing in me even when I made a mess out of things.

Then there's the time I lost my temper and punched a hole in my bedroom door. You didn't say much when you discovered it, but neither did you replace the door. You left it like it was, you said, to remind me how destructive anger can be. You finally got around to replacing it last year, but for more than twenty-five years I had to view the evidence of my childish tantrum every time we came home for a visit.

Had you spanked me, you would have been justified, but even the most painful spanking is soon forgotten. Mother suggested that I buy a new door with my own money, but you vetoed that idea also. To your way of thinking, nothing would make a more lasting impression than viewing that fist-sized hole for years to come.

How right you were. I never saw that hole but what I vowed to control my temper. Requiring me to memorize Proverbs 16:32 ("Better a patient man than a warrior, a man who controls his temper than one who takes a city.") was a good idea too.

One last thing. As a boy I desperately hungered for your praise, but felt that I seldom received it. To this day, I cannot remember a single time when you told me that I was a gifted writer or that you were proud of me, but I know you are. I now realize that, while you may not be able to tell me, you tell everyone else. And when you sell my books to your friends and co-workers, that's the highest compliment of all.

Nonetheless, I vowed that I would be different with my children; I vowed that I would heap praise upon them. Guess what? Although I am truly a proud father, like you, I find it nearly impossible to verbalize my feelings. I can only hope that Jeffery and Karen know how I feel.

Thanks again, Dad, for all your love and wisdom. Whatever I have accomplished, and whatever I am as a man and a father, I owe to you.

Your Loving Son,

Folding the letter, you put it into an envelope, address it and stamp it. Yes, you reluctantly admit, your father could have done better in some areas. Still, you are sure that he did the best he could with what he had.

In truth, that's all any of us can do, and it's enough.

Hopefully, Jeffery will be as understanding with your shortcomings as you are with your father's. If not now, in the white-hot heat of youthful idealism, then maybe later when he is more in touch with his own humanity.

CHAPTER

8

Celebrating Life

"When your dad goes the way of all flesh, you will not grieve over what might have been, rather you will thank God for all the good times you had. You are going to celebrate life!"

Chapter 8

∽

Celebrating Life

Your seemingly indestructible father undergoes two major surgeries in the space of three weeks. The first is double by-pass, open-heart surgery. Then, three weeks later, he has his gall bladder removed.

You aren't able to get a flight until late evening, and it is well past ten o'clock when you finally make it to the hospital. Your father acknowledges your presence, but that is about all he can manage before succumbing to the pain medication. About midnight, you leave your mother to her bedside vigil and drive "home" to the house where you grew up.

Opening the trunk to get your bag, you see your dad's toolbox and coveralls – symbols of his strength and resourcefulness. There wasn't anything he couldn't fix.

In the living room you encounter his favorite chair, a Lazy-Boy recliner covered in a wool plaid. Now, it becomes a haunting symbol of his sickness. How many nights has he spent here, unable to sleep, alone with the darkness and his pain?

A deep sadness settles over you. You try to reason it away. You are tired and lonely, you tell yourself, the house is empty. Your sadness isn't fooled. You are face to face with your own mortality, and your father's.

Although you are tired, you can't sleep, so you wander through the empty house listening to the stillness. How different from your childhood when four kids created a constant commotion. How different from other trips home, holidays and vacations when the house rang with laughter and love, when grandchildren were everywhere underfoot.

You sit in your dad's favorite chair and cry. You try not to, but you can't help it.

Yet, even in your sadness, you realize that you have much to be thankful for. In this trying experience, you and your father have shared on a deeper level than ever before. Neither of you wanted a single affirming word unshared, any feeling of love unexpressed.

You remember holding his hand the day before his open-heart surgery and recall the closeness you felt. The way he blinked to hold back his tears when he told you all the things he had wanted to do for your mother and hadn't got to, at least not yet. Some improvements on the house and a trip to Hawaii. After a while, he fell asleep, and you were left with your thoughts and the realization of how much you love that special man you call Dad.

Alone in the house, you have a choice. You can entertain either your fears or your memories. You choose the latter.

The first thing that comes to mind is something you have been told rather than something of which you have a conscious memory. Your father has always been an avid reader, and when you were just a baby you would sit in his lap, perfectly still, for hours while he read.

Now, sitting in his favorite chair with a stack of books at your elbow, you think of that fact and realize that your own love for books might very well have been born right there in his arms. Even today you think of a good book as a trusted friend, and you associate reading with happiness and love. Is it not possible that those warm feelings are a carry-over of the love and security you found in your father's embrace?

Now your mind leaps ahead twenty years. You and your wife are serving as the pastors of a small church in Colorado. Your folks live nearly 1,100 miles away, yet they drive all night to share their granddaughter's first Christmas. She is only seven months old, and your wife has dressed her in striped pajamas and a tiny Santa's cap.

After the arrival of your parents, in the wee hours of the morning, you immediately exchange gifts — after lots of kisses and hugs, that is. Later that day, you go ice skating on a pond swept clean of snow by bitterly cold winds, high in the Rockies. Then you take turns riding a toboggan down the mountainside at speeds no one in his right mind would ever attempt. Miraculously, no one is hurt, and you return to the house for Christmas leftovers and childhood memories, relived with a relish known only to happy families.

Back again in the present, your mind goes to your childhood. This time to the night you were called to preach.

You were barely thirteen years old, and when you told your dad, he gave you just enough affirmation to let you know how proud he was, but not nearly enough to make you think more highly of yourself than you should have. Then he gave you some of the wisest counsel you have ever received.

"Son," he said, "let's keep your call a secret between the two of us for a while. When you start preaching or begin preparation for the ministry, you can make it public."

You accepted his counsel that night, without question, because you trusted him. Now, these many years later, you recognize his wisdom. If your call had proved to be nothing but an emotional experience, and you had already announced it, you might have felt obligated to continue just to save face.

This reliving of the past goes on all night long as you toss fitfully, unable to sleep, with only God and your memories to keep you company.

Along about dawn, you realize that even if your father dies, you will still have much for which to be thankful. The thirty-eight years you have shared together have contained enough love and laughter for two or three lifetimes. No one could ever take your dad's place. You understand that better than ever now, but you also realize that you will always have the memories and the God your dad made more real to you than life itself.

No matter what happens, whether your father lives or dies, you decide you are going to celebrate life, and when you do, you discover that the Lord of Life is present and celebrating with you!

You know now better how to prepare for that inevitable moment we all must face.

When your dad goes the way of all flesh, you will not grieve over what might have been, rather you will thank God for all the good times you had. You are going to celebrate life!

Your Dad would want it that way.

That doesn't mean you won't grieve, or that you won't miss him. It simply means that he can't ever be totally gone as long as you have the memories of the life he so freely shared with you and all of his family.

Epilogue

I am forty-eight years old now, and I realize that there are many things I may never accomplish in this life.

For instance, I may never write a book that sells a million copies. I may never serve as pastor of a church of several thousand members, and I will probably never be elected to an important position in my denomination.

There was a time when all of that was very important to me. Not anymore. I still want to be the very best I can be in everything I do, but I am no longer driven by temporal symbols of success. Achievements of that nature, while gratifying, pale in comparison with the true achievements of life — the shaping of the faith and character of my family.

I am convinced that when we stand before God, at the final judgment, He will not ask us about our honors and the awards we have won. He will not ask us about the degrees we have earned, or the wealth we have amassed. Rather, He will ask, "Where are the children I entrusted to you?"

In light of that fact, the greatest reward a man can ever hope to receive, this side of eternity, is to see his children cherishing the faith which he entrusted to them. And to watch with thanksgiving as they make the family's spiritual traditions their own and a vital part of their children's lives.

May God continue to guide, strengthen and encourage each of us as we seek to fulfill our vital role as Christian fathers.

Other books by Richard Exley
are available from your local bookstore.

Straight From the Heart for Mom

Straight From the Heart for Couples

Straight From the Heart for Graduates

*How to Be a Man of Character
in a World of Compromise*

Marriage in the Making

The Making of a Man

Abortion

Blue-Collar Christianity

Life's Bottom Line

Perils of Power

The Rhythm of Life

When You Lose Someone You Love

*The Other God –
Seeing God as He Really Is*

The Painted Parable

To contact the author, write:

Richard Exley
P.O. Box 54744
Tulsa, Oklahoma 74155

*Please include your prayer requests
when you write.*

HONOR
BOOKS

Tulsa, Oklahoma